The Bear Who Wouldn't Share

Written and illustrated by
Jonathan Allen

Rigby
A Harcourt Achieve Imprint

www.Rigby.com
1-800-531-5015

It was Bear's birthday.

Granny Bear had baked him a cake.

Invite your friends to tea, young Bear.

I made this cake for you to share.

Bear was horrified.

SHARE? But if I ask my friends to tea, there won't be *so much* cake for me!

But then he thought of a plan...

I'd like to see my friends a lot, but I fancy that cake more. I know! I'll only ask those friends who won't fit through my door!

Bear was just about
to eat the first slice
when he heard
a knock at the door.

My friends have come
to share my cake.
Just listen to
the noise they make!

Bear was on his fourth slice when he heard another knock.

My friends are knocking at the door.
I'd better quickly eat some more!

It was Giraffe and
Elephant at the door.

Push! Shove!
Push some more!
Oof! Bear, we can't fit
through your door!

Oh dear, oh dear,
that's just too bad.
This cake's the best
I've ever had.

Bear had nearly
finished the cake
when he heard
another knock.

My friends are here,
but just too late.
They'll only get
an empty plate!

Bear grinned and finished eating the last crumbs.

Meanwhile, his friends were having their own party outside.

The cake's all gone.

I'm really done.

Now I'll go out

to join the fun!

Just then Granny Bear
came to see how
the party was going.

I *see* Bear's friends,
but where is Bear?
And where's that cake
I made to share?

21

Bear suddenly felt very left out.